POLYDRON MATHSWORKS 3

Shape Investigations and Problem Solving

Peter Patilla, Ann Sawyer, Paul Broadbent

 LDA

 POLYDRON

POLYDRON MATHSWORKS 3
LD 898
ISBN 1 85503 216 3

© Text: Peter Patilla, Paul Broadbent, Ann Sawyer
© Illustrations: Brian Hoskin

Photography: DLP Communications
First published under licence from Polydron UK Ltd. 1994
All rights reserved

LDA, Duke Street, Wisbech, Cambs, PE13 2AE, England

THE POLYDRON CONSTRUCTION SYSTEM

Polydron Mathsworks 3 is designed for use with the Polydron geometric construction system.
For further information about Polydron or to order components contact:

Polydron UK Ltd, 11 Scotia Close, Brackmills, Northampton, NN4 7HR, England

CONTENTS

contents

introduction

Polydron Mathsworks 3 is a resource offering exciting starting points for investigation and problem solving with aspects of Shape and Space. The activities complement those contained in Mathsworks 1.

The activities in this pack are designed for pupils working at Levels 2–5 of the National Curriculum for England, Wales and Northern Ireland and Levels B–D of the Scottish Guidelines.

Using the Book

This book has been written as a resource bank of ideas for teachers to support their teaching of Shape and Space in the primary classroom. It has been designed for use in conjunction with Polydron shapes and contains a variety of photocopiable resource sheets.

There are ten shape topics, each supported by a page of teacher's notes and seven activity sheets. The teacher's notes include:

▲ comments about individual investigations and problems
▲ teaching points
▲ further activities in the form of challenges
▲ links where activities support the Mathsworks 2 posters.

The Copymaster sheets

There are three types of copymaster sheet:

▲ The photocopiable activity sheets which are starting points for investigations or problem solving tasks. They are presented in a variety of formats and can be completed in any order.
▲ The information sheets which can be copied as a class resource or given to pupils as part of their mathematical dictionary. When pupils come upon a new word concerned with shape they can refer to the information sheets as a first step.
▲ At the back of the book there is a collection of recording sheets for use in conjunction with the activities as appropriate.

Organisation and Management

No particular classroom organisation has been assumed. Pupils can work in groups, pairs, or individually, as the teacher determines.

It is useful for the pupils to create a 'Maths Folder' in which to store their activity sheets and any other related work.

At the back of this book is a photocopiable sheet which can be used for the cover of a pupil's folder.

Using Polydron Shapes

The following Polydron shapes will give opportunities to achieve some exciting results both with the resource book and the Polydron Mathsworks 2 posters.

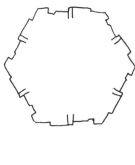
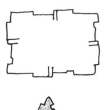

The Mathematics

Encourage pupils to talk about and explain what they have been doing.
Polydron Mathsworks includes the following areas:

Using and applying mathematics/problem solving & enquiry

Mathematical processes can be encouraged and extended.

Starting

▲ exploring the task to identify and interpret what is needed
▲ considering what might be relevant
▲ deciding how to proceed

Doing

▲ implementing strategies
▲ coming to conclusions
▲ evaluating what has been done

Reporting

▲ using a variety of ways
▲ mathematical communication

Pupils will have the opportunity to:

▲ use mathematics as part of practical tasks
▲ talk about their work and respond to questions
▲ select what is needed to work on a task
▲ respond to 'what if' questions
▲ find ways of overcoming difficulties
▲ use mathematical language and terminology

Shape & space/position and movement

Range of shapes

▲ talking about shapes and models
▲ classifying shapes
▲ identifying and naming shapes
▲ creating or copying 3D structures
▲ using mathematical terms to describe models
▲ exploring the properties of 2D and 3D shapes

Position and movement

▲ using prepositions
▲ using angles: opening, closing and turning

Symmetry

▲ balanced shapes
▲ symmetrical models

Measurement

Length

▲ comparison of size
▲ scale

Angle

▲ early ideas of estimation
▲ right angles
▲ concave and convex

Algebra/patterns and relationships

Patterns

▲ continuing sequences of colours and shapes
▲ exploring and developing repeating patterns
▲ exploring and developing continuous patterns

introduction

information

These seven information sheets can be used for identification and classification of 2D and 3D shapes.

Teaching Points

▲ These sheets can be photocopied and used as part of a pupil's mathematical folder. Encourage pupils to find out information about shapes for themselves.

▲ The classification of shapes develops from general terms to the very specific. A very important way of classifying is by the use of the general polygon term – 3-sided, 4-sided, 5-sided ...

▲ Introduce the correct terms for shapes (such as polygon, pyramid, prism...) so that it becomes part of your pupils' everyday language.

Some of the Polydron shapes have all their sides the same length whilst others have short sides and long sides.

The longer side is the same length as the diagonal of the Polydron square.

Long sides will only clip onto long sides and not onto short sides.

It is often easier to clip the shapes togther when they are placed flat on the table or desk top.

3 and 4 Sided Polygons

equilateral triangle
3 equal sides

right-angled isosceles triangle
2 equal sides

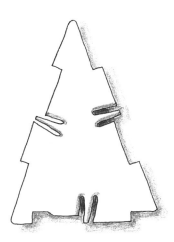

isosceles triangle
2 equal sides

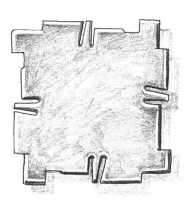

square
4 equal sides and 4 right angles

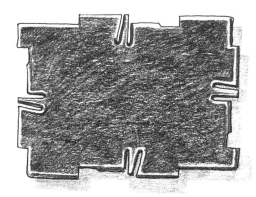

rectangle
opposite sides equal and 4 right angles

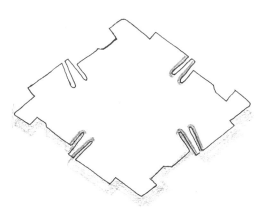

rhombus
4 equal sides and 0 right angles

information 1

Polygons with more than 4 sides

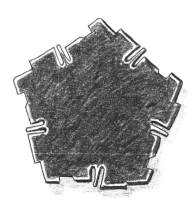

pentagon
5-sided shape

hexagon
6-sided shape

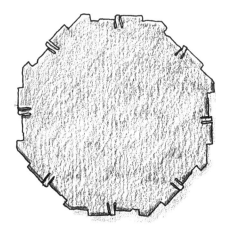

octagon
8-sided shape

Prisms

The shape of the end faces is used to describe most prisms.

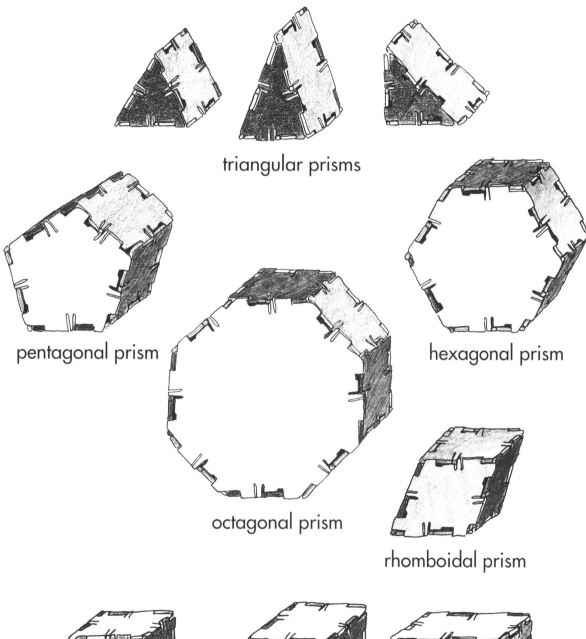

triangular prisms

pentagonal prism

hexagonal prism

octagonal prism

rhomboidal prism

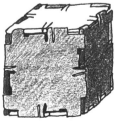

cube

a cube has 6 square faces

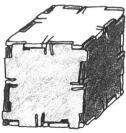

cuboids

a cuboid has 6 rectangular faces
or 4 rectangular and 2 square faces

information 4

Pyramids

Pyramids have polygon bases and triangular sides which meet at a point.

tetrahedrons

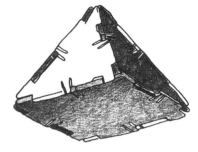

square based pyramid

rectangular based pyramid

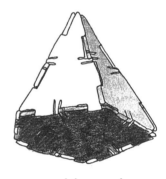

pentagonal based pyramid

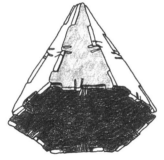

hexagonal based pyramid

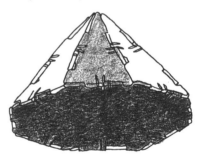

octagonal based pyramid

open pyramids
have a face missing

some pyramids
lean to one side

truncated pyramids
have a corner cut off

Platonic Shapes

The faces of the platonic shapes are all identical regular polygons.
All the faces meet at the same angle.

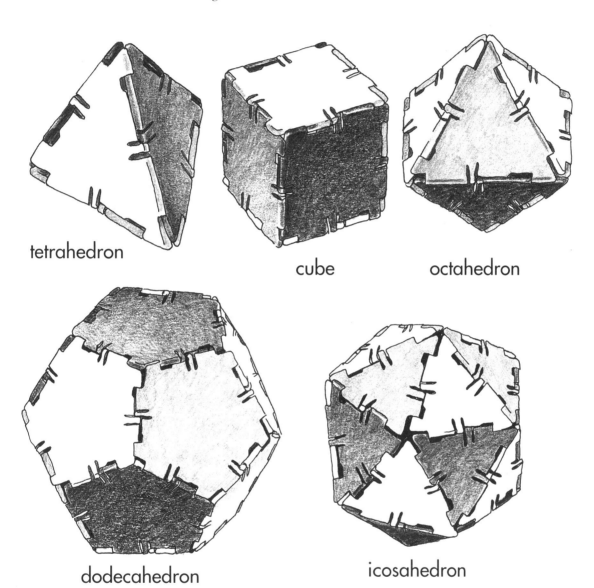

tetrahedron

cube

octahedron

dodecahedron

icosahedron

Name	Faces
regular tetrahedron	4 equilateral triangles
cube	6 squares
regular octahedron	8 equilateral triangles
regular dodecahedron	12 regular pentagons
regular icosahedron	20 equilateral triangles

information 6

Polygons

Polygons are any closed 2D shape which has straight sides.
A regular polygon has all its sides the same length and all its angles the same size.

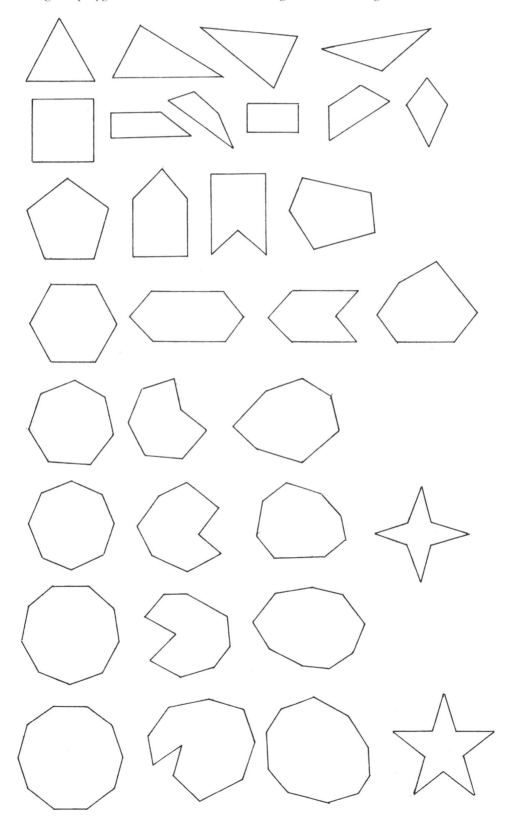

Polyhedra

A polyhedron is any 3D shape which has flat faces.
Several can be called either polyhedra or polyhedrons.

Polyhedra with ...

4 faces	tetrahedron	
6 faces	hexahedron	
8 faces	octahedron	
10 faces	decahedron	
12 faces	dodecahedron	
20 faces	icosahedron	

Parts of a 3D shape

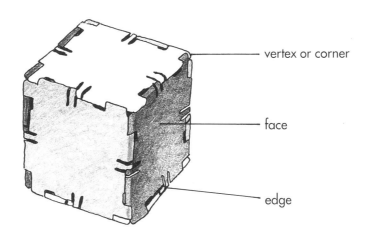

vertex or corner

face

edge

Outlines

These activities involve pupils clipping Polydron shapes together to match the simple outline on the activity sheet.

Each outline can be made by using either:

> several of a single shape, or
> several of two shapes.

Once the outline has been created pupils draw and label the shapes they used inside the outline. Freehand drawings are adequate for the recording.

For each activity, new outlines are made by rearranging the same set of shapes. Some of the new outlines can be drawn on the back of the activity sheet.

Teaching Opportunities

As the same set of Polydron pieces is being used to make different arrangements, each shape created will have the same area. Discuss conservation of area.

Once a collection of shapes has been created encourage pupils to sort and classify them. Reasons for sorting can include:

> symmetrical shapes
> concave shapes
> convex shapes
> shapes with sides of equal length
> shapes which will tessellate
> shapes which have a right angled corner
> number of sides

There are two possible lengths of side on the Polydron pieces: long and short. The longer side matches the diagonal on the square. Discuss perimeters.

Challenges

Set challenges such as:

> Make a shape which has as many sides as possible.
> Make a shape which has as few sides as possible.
> Make up an outline for someone else to fill in.
> Make outlines which have symmetry.

This can be linked to Poster 5 from Polydron Mathsworks 2: Making Symmetrical Shapes.

Outlines 1

Make a shape which has an outline like this.

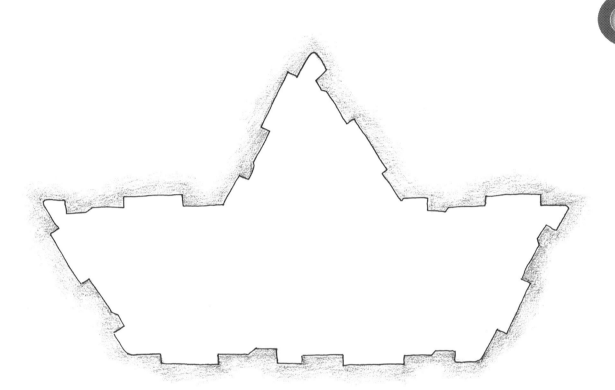

Draw the shapes you used in the outline.

Make your own different outline using the same pieces.

Draw the new outline on the back of this sheet.

POLYDRON

Outlines 2

Make a shape which has an outline like this.

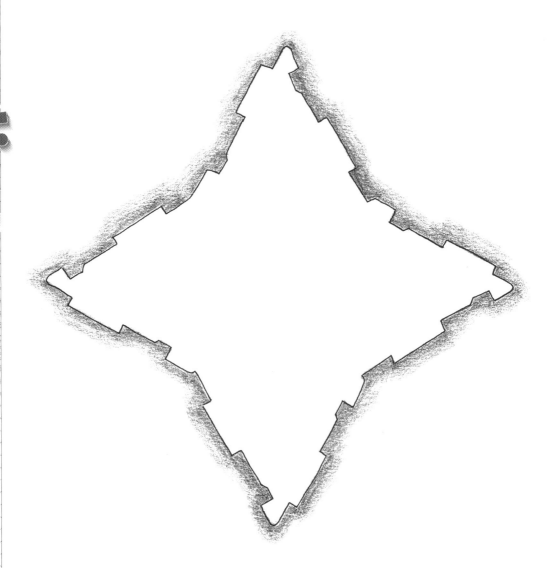

Draw the shapes you used in the outline.

Make your own different outline using the same pieces.

Draw the new outline on the back of this sheet.

LDA

POLYDRON

Outlines 3

Make a shape which has an outline like this.

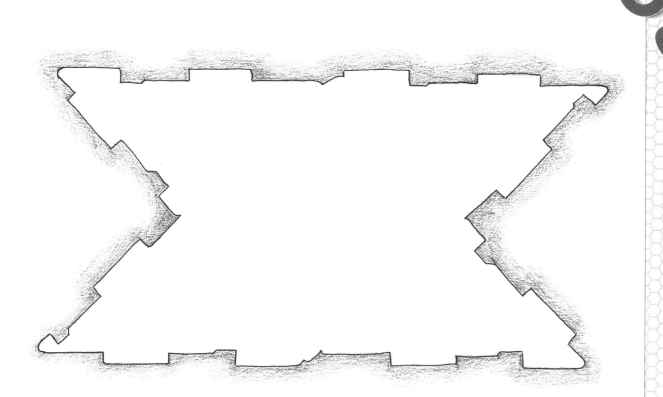

Draw the shapes you used in the outline.

Make your own different outline using the same pieces.

Draw the new outline on the back of this sheet.

POLYDRON

Outlines 4

Make a shape which has an outline like this.

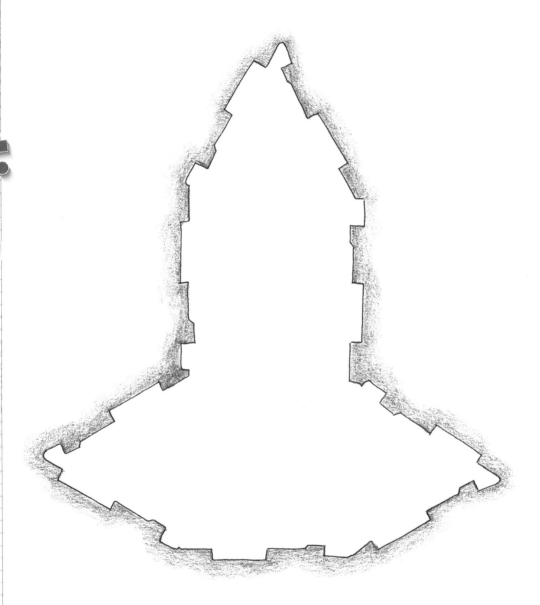

Draw the shapes you used in the outline.

Make your own different outline using the same pieces.

Draw the new outline on the back of this sheet.

LDA

POLYDRON

Outlines 5

Make a shape which has an ouline like this.

Draw the shapes you used in the outline.

Make your own different outline using the same pieces.

Draw the new outline on the back of this sheet.

Outlines 6

Make a shape which has an outline like this.

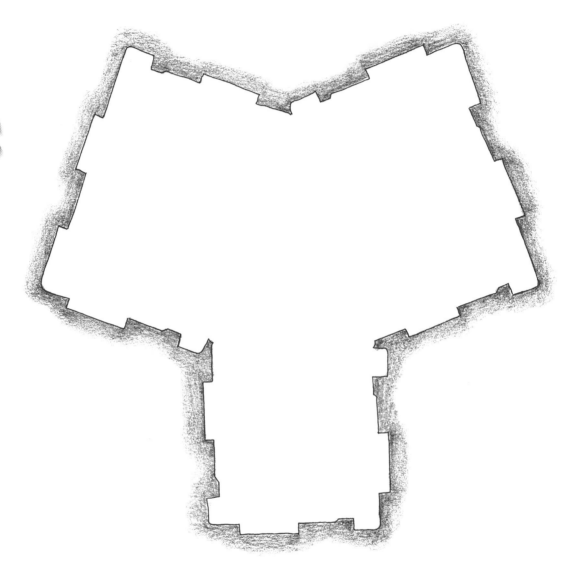

Draw the shapes you used in the outline.

Make your own different outline using the same pieces.

Draw the new outline on the back of this sheet.

LDA

POLYDRON

Outlines 7

Make a shape which has an outline like this.

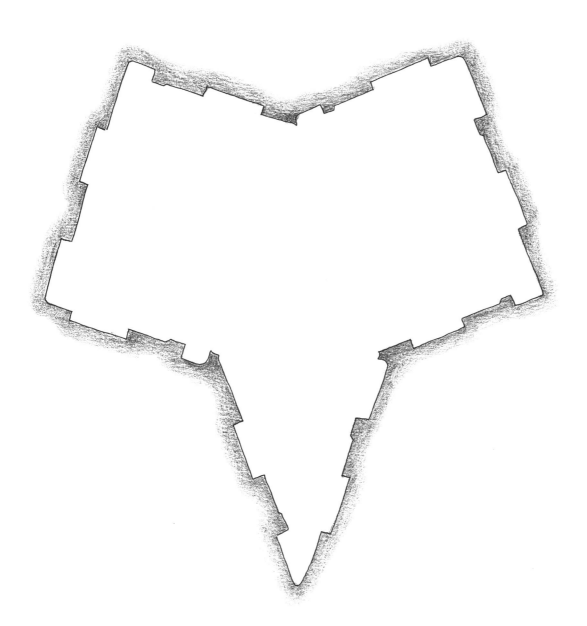

Draw the shapes you used in the outline.

Make your own different outline using the same pieces.

Draw the new outline on the back of this sheet.

LDA

POLYDRON

Triangles

These activities involve pupils clipping triangles together to create larger triangles as well as other polygons.

The activities lend themselves to developing appropriate shape vocabulary, particularly relating to triangles –

Describing sides: equilateral
                                isosceles
                                scalene
Describing angles: right angled
                                acute
                                obtuse

Teaching Opportunities

Discuss the fact that right angled triangles can also be isosceles.

All polygons can be described by the number of their sides:
        3-sided shapes, 4-sided shapes, 5-sided shapes, ...
and by general names:
        triangles, quadrilaterals, pentagons, ...

Rotate and flip the interlocked shapes to develop ideas of position and symmetry.

Challenges

Sort and describe shapes using attributes such as:

        convex shapes
        concave shapes
        right angled shapes
        symmetrical shapes
        shapes which tessellate

These activities can be used in conjunction with Poster 1: Making Growing Patterns and Poster 3: Making Colour Patterns from Mathsworks 2.

Making 4-Sided Shapes

You need 4 right angled triangles.

Make a rectangle.

Make other 4-sided shapes, with the triangles

Draw your shapes.

Triangles

Exploring Polygons

You need 4 equilateral triangles.

Make different polygons using these 4 triangles.

Draw some of your polygons on this chart.

3-sided	4-sided
5-sided	**6-sided**

LDA   POLYDRON

Growing Triangles

Make this pattern using two colours.

Continue the pattern for the next 2 shapes.

Fill in the chart.

Triangle	1	2	3	4	5
Colour 1					
Colour 2					
Total					

Write about any patterns you notice.

LDA

POLYDRON

Take 2 Triangles ...

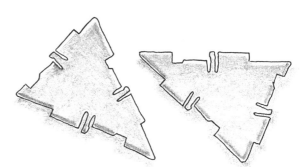

Clip pairs of triangles together to make different quadrilaterals.

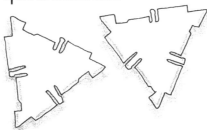 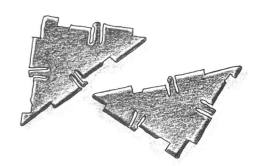

Draw and name the quadrilaterals you have made.

LDA

POLYDRON

Changing Shapes

Make triangles by clipping different Polydron pieces together.

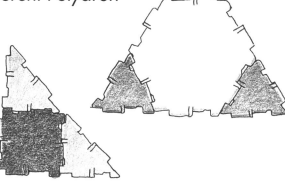

Draw the shapes you used.

Show how you made each triangle.

Take 5 Triangles ...

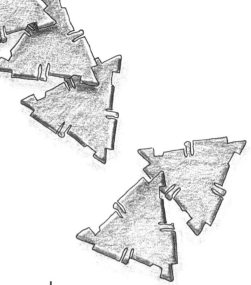

Clip 5 equilateral triangles together to make different polygons.

Draw and name the polygons you have made.

LDA

POLYDRON

Line Symmetry

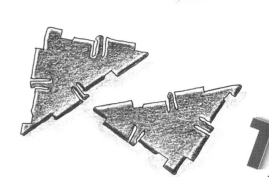

Make polygons by clipping together pairs of triangles.

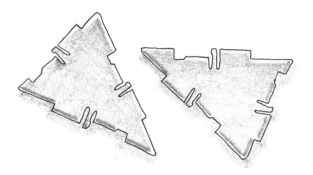

Draw some of your polygons on the Carroll diagram.

Line Symmetry	Line Symmetry ✗

teacher's notes

Squares

These activities involve pupils using squares to explore patterns and shapes.

Recording forms an important part of these activities. Additional recording sheets can be found on pages 94–95.

Teaching Opportunities

Look at tiling patterns using squares in the environment; discuss the properties of squares.

Rotate and flip the interlocked shapes to develop ideas of position and symmetry.

Use the recorded results to discuss :

- ▲ shape classification
- ▲ properties of shape
- ▲ number patterns

For example, for activities 1 and 2 :

Sort the set of shapes.

Challenges

Try using different Polydron shapes to make squares.

Make models to hold 5, 6, 7 … square Polydron pieces.

These activities can be used in conjunction with Poster 9: Making Tessellations, from Mathsworks 2.

Take 4 Squares ...

Clip together 4 squares to see how many different shapes you can make.

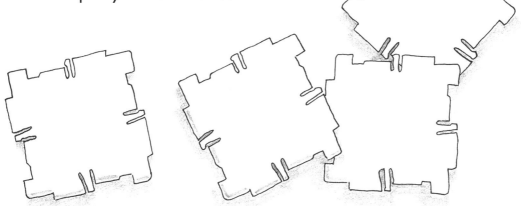

Draw all the shapes you can make with 4 squares.

LDA

POLYDRON

Squares

Take 5 Squares ...

Clip together 5 squares to see
how many different shapes
you can make.

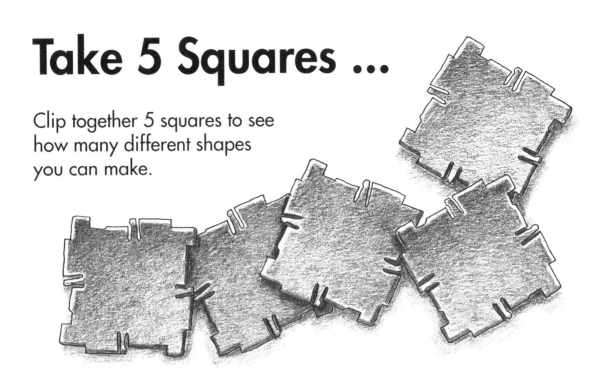

Draw the shapes you can make with 5 squares.

LDA

POLYDRON

Closed Boxes

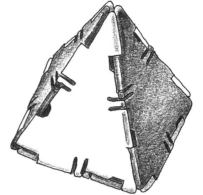

Make a square based pyramid.

Make a box from Polydron pieces to hold your pyramid.

Draw the pieces you need to make your box.

Squares

CHALLENGE

Fit as many Polydron models as possible inside the box.

Square Panels

Make a two colour panel from 6 squares.

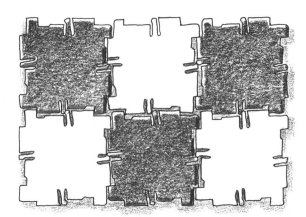

Rearrange the squares to make different panels.

Make sure the panels are different even when turned or flipped over.

Draw the different panels on the grid.

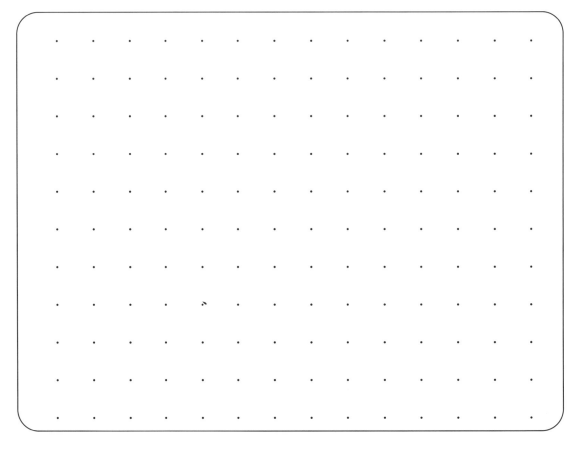

LDA

POLYDRON

Symmetrical Shapes

Make a symmetrical shape using different coloured squares.

The colour pattern must also be symmetrical.

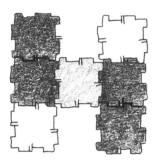 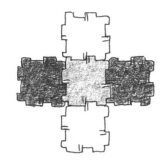 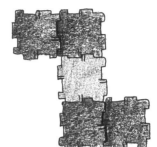

Draw some of your patterns.

LDA

POLYDRON

Area and Perimeter

Make this pattern using squares:

Continue the pattern for the next 2 shapes.

Fill in the chart.

Number of squares	Perimeter	Area

Write about any patterns you notice.

LDA

POLYDRON

Tiling Patterns

Make these 4 squares using right angled triangles.

Clip the squares together
to make this pattern.

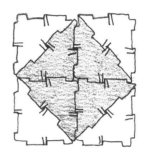

Rearrange the squares to make more tiling patterns.

Draw them here.

LDA

POLYDRON

teacher's notes

Unfolding

These activities involve pupils clipping Polydron pieces together to make the 3D shape shown on the activity sheet.

Pupils are then asked to open out the shape and to sketch the net. Freehand drawings are adequate for recording.

For each activity the shape should be opened up in as many ways as the child can find and then each net sketched. Where there are many possible nets some of these can be sketched on the back of the activity sheet.

The shapes are:

Unfolding 1: cube
Unfolding 2: cuboid
Unfolding 3: square based pyramid
Unfolding 4: triangular prism
Unfolding 5: pentagonal prism
Unfolding 6: hexagonal prism
Unfolding 7: tetrahedron

Teaching opportunities

Each shape has a range of possible nets. The information sheets on pages 7–11 can be used to find the names of the shapes.

Look for both line and rotational symmetry in the nets.

Compare the nets made to see which are reflections or rotations of others.

Compare the perimeters of the nets. Are they always the same or different?

Discuss the surface area of each shape.

Challenges

Make each shape using different pieces, such as:

a cube from right angled triangles
a cuboid from squares
a hexagonal prism from triangles

Open out these shapes to find some more nets.

Make this shape.

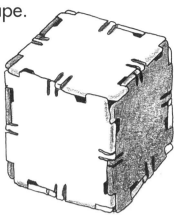

It is called a _____

Open it out and sketch the net.

Fold the net up again. Unfold to make a different net.

See how many nets you can make.

Unfolding

Make this shape.

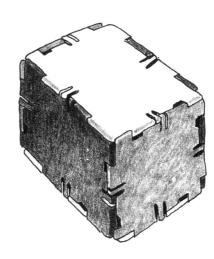

It is called a

_____

Open it out and sketch the net.

Fold the net up again. Unfold to make a different net.

See how many nets you can make.

POLYDRON

Make this shape.

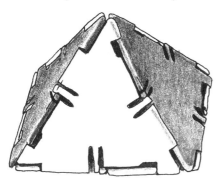

It is called a _____

Open it out and sketch the net.

Fold the net up again. Unfold to make a different net.

See how many nets you can make.

LDA

POLYDRON

Make this shape.

It is called a _____

Open it out and sketch the net.

Fold the net up again. Unfold to make a different net.

See how many nets you can make.

LDA

POLYDRON

Make this shape.

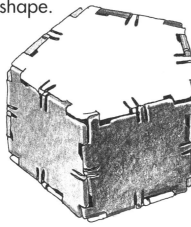

It is called a _____

Open it out and sketch the net.

Fold the net up again. Unfold to make a different net.

See how many nets you can make.

LDA

POLYDRON

Make this shape.

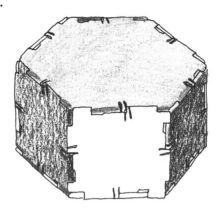

It is called a

_____

Open it out and sketch the net.

Fold the net up again. Unfold to make a different net.

See how many nets you can make.

Make this shape.

It is called a _____

Open it out and sketch the net.

Fold the net up again. Unfold to make a different net.

See how many nets you can make.

LDA

POLYDRON

teacher's notes

Folding

These activities involve pupils clipping together Polydron pieces to copy the net outline shown on the activity sheet. Then the net is then folded up to make a 3-D shape.

The shapes are

> Folding 1: cube
> Folding 2: cuboid
> Folding 3: square base pyramid
> Folding 4: triangular prism
> Folding 5: pentagonal prism
> Folding 6: hexagonal prism
> Folding 7: tetrahedron.

Pupils are asked to open up the shape again to make a different net. Freehand drawings are adequate for the recording. Some of the outlines can be drawn on the back of the activity sheet or the recording sheets on pages 94 and 95.

Teaching opportunities

Explain the term 'net'.

The information sheets on pages 7–11 can be used for finding the names of the shapes.

Encourage the pupils to find as many different nets as possible for each shape.

Because the same set of Polydron pieces is being used to make different nets, each net will have the same surface area.

Discuss conservation of area.

Challenges

Look at the drawings of the nets and identify which have line and which have rotational symmetry.

Compare the nets to see which are reflections or rotations of others.

Fold this into a closed 3-D shape.

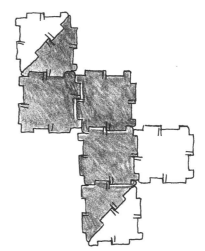

It is called a _____

Now carefully unfold it to make a different net.

Draw the new net.

How many different nets can you find?

Folding

LDA

POLYDRON

Fold this into a closed 3-D shape.

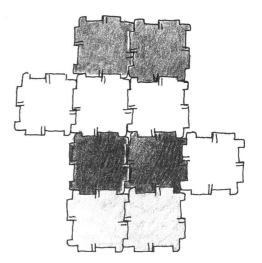

It is called a _____

Now carefully unfold it to make a different net.

Draw the net.

How many different nets can you find?

LDA

POLYDRON

Fold this into a closed 3-D shape.

It is called a _____

Now carefully unfold it to make a different net.

Draw the net.

Fold the net up again.

Unfold and draw.

POLYDRON

Fold this into a closed 3-D shape.

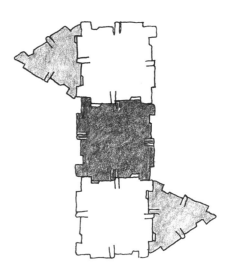

It is called a _____

Now carefully unfold it to make a different net.

Draw the net.

Fold the net up again.

Unfold and draw.

LDA

POLYDRON

Fold this into a closed 3-D shape.

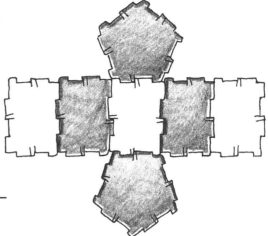

It is called a _____

Now carefully unfold it to make a different net.

Draw the net.

How many different nets can you find?

POLYDRON

Folding

Fold this into a closed 3-D shape.

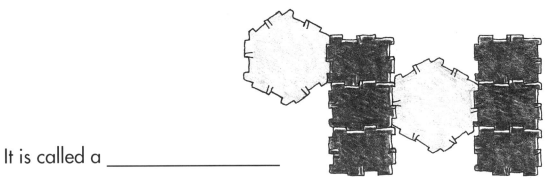

It is called a _____

Now carefully unfold it to make a different net.

Draw the net.

How many different nets can you find?

POLYDRON

Fold this into a closed 3-D shape.

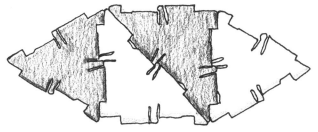

It is called a _____

Now carefully unfold it to make a different net.

Draw the net.

Fold the net up again.

Unfold and draw.

teacher's notes

Making 3-D Shapes

These activities involve pupils in clipping Poydron pieces together to make the named shape on the copymaster. Polydron shapes are limited in this section to equilateral, isosceles and right angled triangles, squares and rectangles.

Before the shape is made, pupils are asked to predict how many of each shape will be needed, then to check their prediction when the shape has been completed. There is a table on each activity sheet for pupil's to complete.

Teaching Opportunities

The information sheets on pages 7–11 can be used for finding an example of the shape.

Challenge

Draw the net before making the shape. Check that the net worked.

Substitute other Polydron pieces so that the shape remains the same.

    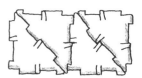

Discuss the properties of the 3D shapes :

No. of edges	Vertices	Faces

Look for symmetry of the 3D shapes.

These activities can be used in conjunction with Poster 7: Making Platonic Solids from Mathsworks 2.

Predict how many of each Polydron piece you will need
to make this.

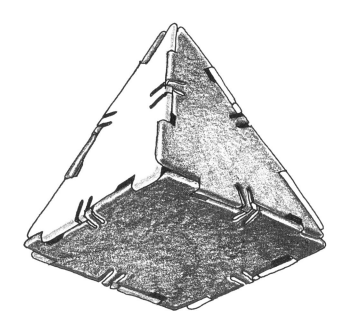

Shape					
Prediction					
Actual					

LDA

POLYDRON

Predict how many of each Polydron piece you will need to make this.

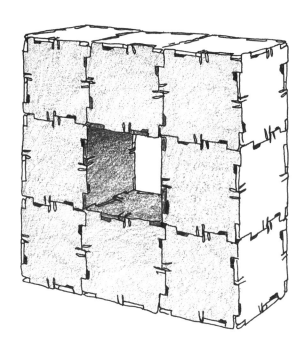

Making 3-D shapes

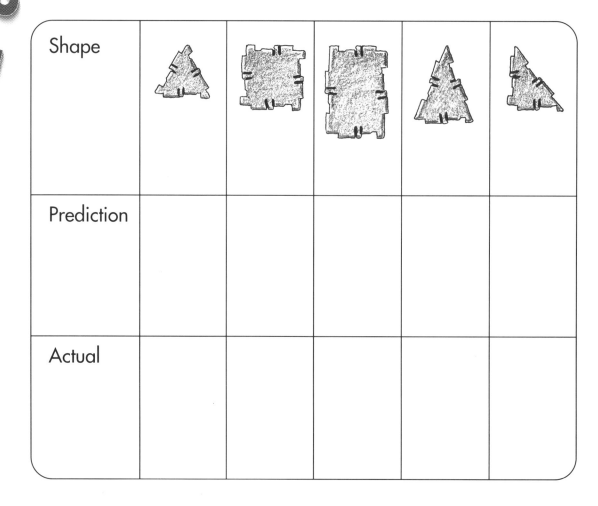

Shape					
Prediction					
Actual					

LDA

POLYDRON

Predict how many of each Polydron piece you will need to make this.

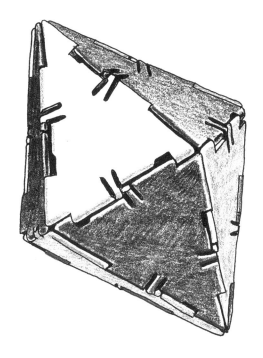

Shape					
Prediction					
Actual					

LDA

POLYDRON

Making 3-D shapes

Predict how many of each Polydron piece you will need to make this.

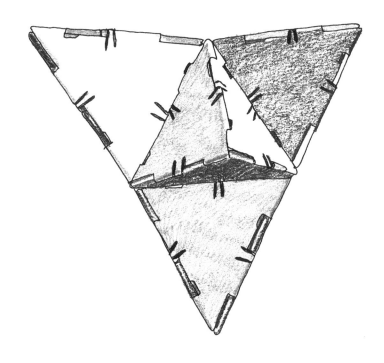

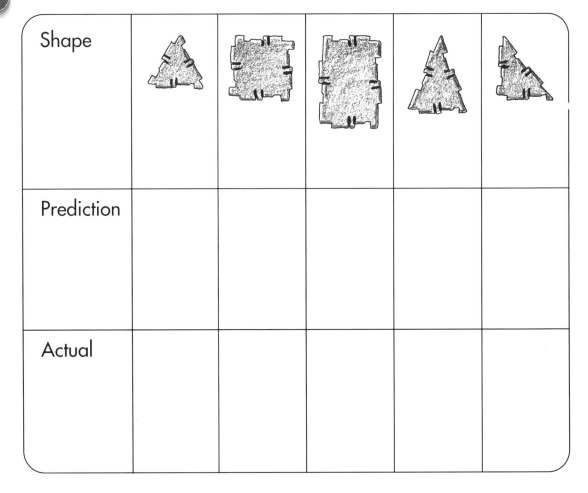

Shape					
Prediction					
Actual					

LDA

POLYDRON

Predict how many of each Polydron piece you will
need to make this.

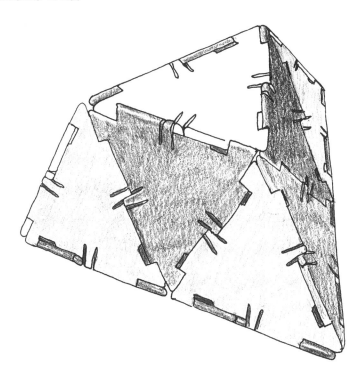

Shape					
Prediction					
Actual					

LDA   POLYDRON

Making 3-D shapes

Predict how many of each Polydron piece you will
need to make this.

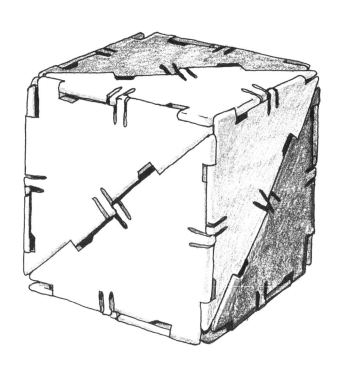

Shape	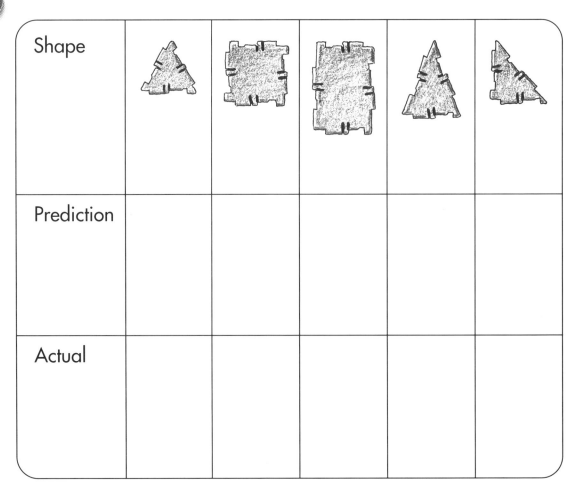				
Prediction					
Actual					

Making 3-D shapes

POLYDRON

Predict how many of each Polydron piece you
will need to make this.

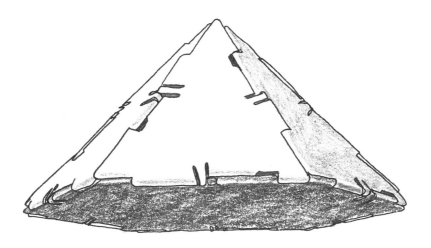

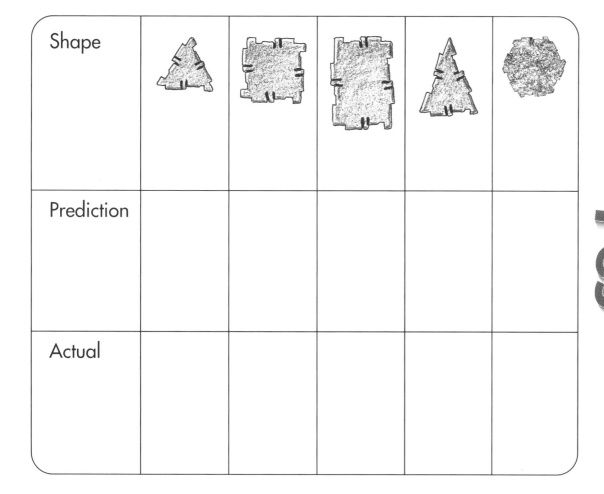

Shape					
Prediction					
Actual					

POLYDRON

Making 3-D shapes

Different Views

These activities involve pupils clipping Polydron pieces together so that the resulting model matches with the view of one or two sides given on the activity sheet

Once the model has been made, the pupils draw another view of the model.

Teaching Opportunities

Encourage pupils to make other models which fit the given views. Make a display showing a range of models which fit the views on one activity sheet. Encourage the children to make other models for the display.

Examine each model for symmetry.

Challenges

Complete an activity sheet using as few Polydron pieces as possible.

Challenge a partner to make a shape from a verbal description.

Top view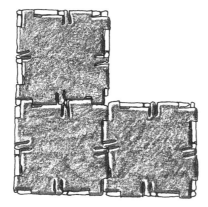

Make a solid model with this top view.

Draw a side view and front view of your model.

Make some more models with the same top view.

LDA

POLYDRON

Top view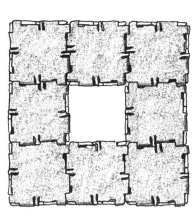

Make a solid model with this top view.

Draw a side view and front view.

Make some more models with the same top view.

Different views

Top view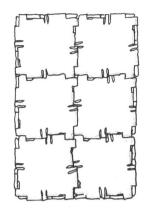

Make a solid model with this top view.

Draw a side view and front view of your model.

Make some more models with the same top view.

LDA

POLYDRON

Top view

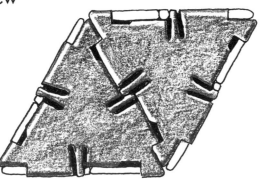

Make a solid model with this top view.

Draw a side view and front view of your model.

Make some more models with the same top view.

POLYDRON

Make a model
with this
end view...

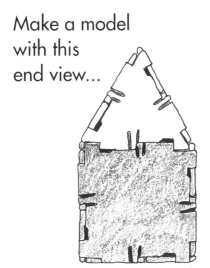

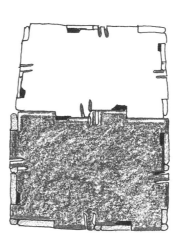

...and this
side view.

Draw the front view of your model.

Make some more models with the same top and side view.

LDA

POLYDRON

Different views

Different views

Make a model
with this
top view...

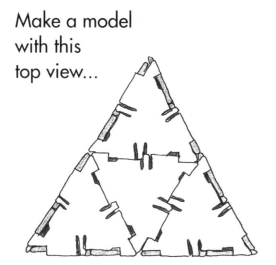

...and this
side view.

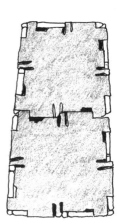

Draw the front view of your model.

Make some more models with the same top and side view.

LDA

POLYDRON

Make a model with this top view...

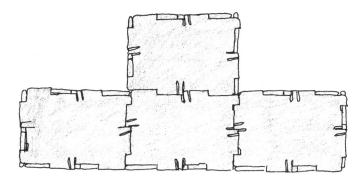

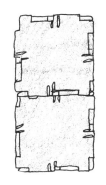

...and this side view.

Draw the front view.

Make some more models with the same top and side view.

Different views

teacher's notes

Faces

These activities focus on the faces of solid shapes.

Teaching Opportunities

Ensure pupils realise that regular polygons must have all their sides and angles equal. If this is not the case then the shape is not regular. They need to appreciate that isosceles triangles, rectangles and rhombuses are not regular shapes.

Discuss ways in which a solid shape can be described, such as:

> number of faces, edges and corners
> the shapes of the faces
> whether all the faces are exactly the same shape and size
> whether the shape is symmetrical

Challenge

Discuss different types of solid shapes such as:

> prisms
> pyramids
> platonic solids

Drawing a complete solid shape can be challenging. The shapes of the faces can be drawn with the number of each indicated.

These activities can be used in conjunction with Poster 12: Faces the Same, from Mathsworks 2.

Colour the regular polygons.

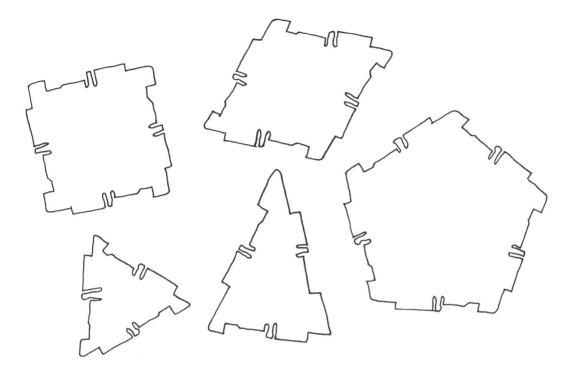

Make a solid shape using only the regular 3-sided shape.

Each face of your solid must be exacty the same.

Write some facts about your solid shape.

LDA

POLYDRON

Colour the regular polygons.

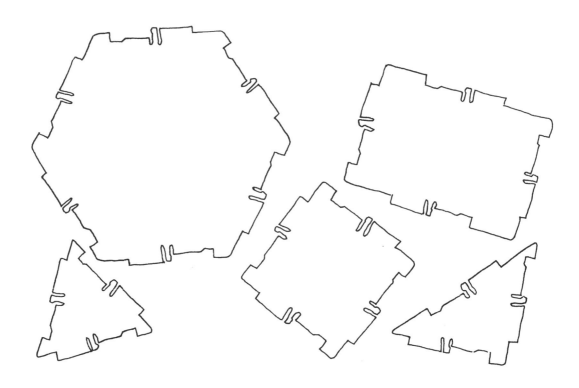

Make a solid shape using only the regular 4-sided shape.

Each face of your solid must be exactly the same.

Write some facts about your solid shape.

Colour the regular polygons.

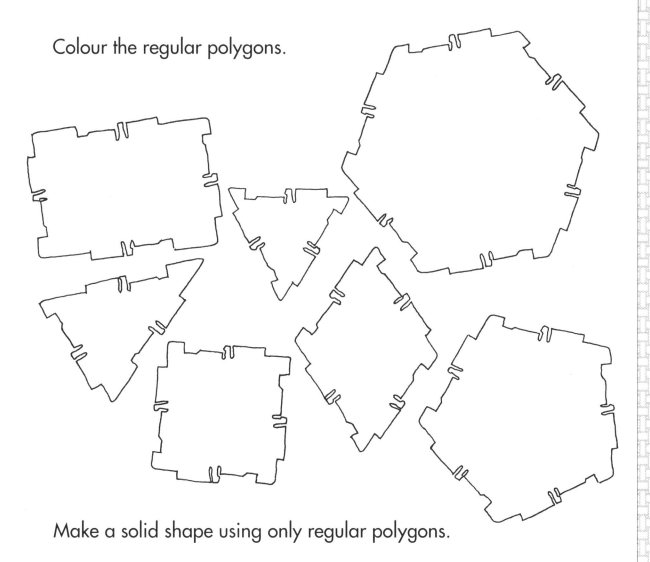

Make a solid shape using only regular polygons.

Write some facts about your solid shape.

LDA

POLYDRON

Colour the irregular polygons.

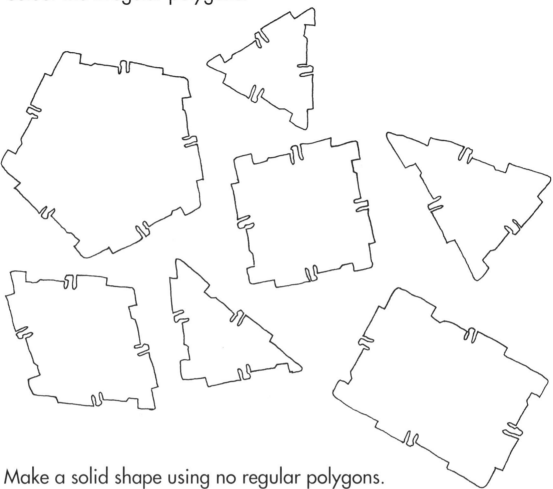

Make a solid shape using no regular polygons.

Write some facts about your solid shape.

LDA

POLYDRON

Clip triangles onto a hexagon to make a trapezium.

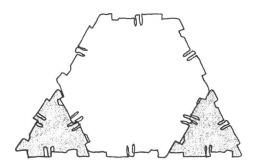

Make a solid shape which has some trapezium faces.

Draw your solid shape and write some facts about it.

Faces

Make a solid shape which has a colour pattern on each face.

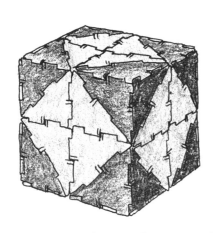 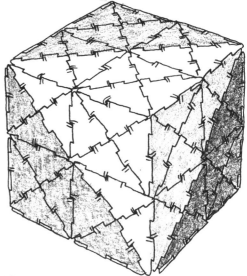

Draw each face of your solid shape.

LDA

POLYDRON

Stellated solids have pyramids coming off each face.

Here is a stellated cube.

Make a stellated cube.

A stellated cube has _____ triangle faces.

Make another stellated shape.

Write its name and some information about it.

Name of shape: _____

Information:

Big Names

These activities involve pupils in learning about special types of solid shapes.

Reassure pupils that making some of the solid shapes can be challenging and not to be discouraged when occasionally they collapse their models. With care all the shapes can be made.

Teaching Opportunities

Discuss the five 'special' solids which are called Platonic Solids:

Tetrahedron

Cube

Octahedron

Dodecahedron

Icosahedron

Look at the faces on each platonic solid – they are all identical regular polygons.

Discuss regular polygons – those hich have all their sides and angles the same size.

Talk about polygons and polyhedra.

▲ polygon means 'many angles'
▲ polyhedra means 'many faces'.

Challenges

Count the number of faces, edges and corners on solid shapes to see whether Euler's rule works:

Faces + Corners = Edges + 2

These activity sheets can be used in conjunction with Poster 7: Platonic Solids, from Polydron Mathsworks 2.

The Octahedron

Here is a drawing of an octahedron.

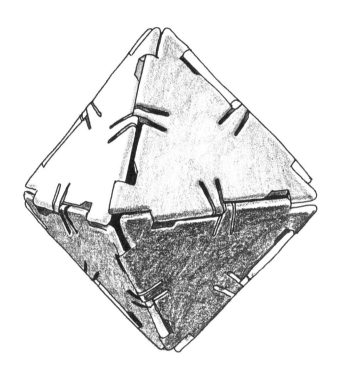

Make an octahedron using Polydron shapes.

An octahedron has:

_____ equilateral triangle faces

_____ corners

_____ edges

LDA

POLYDRON

The Dodecahedron

Here is a drawing of a dodecahedron.

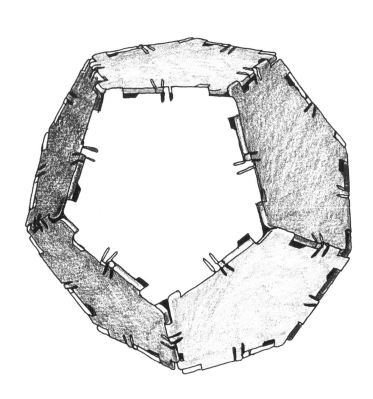

Make a dodecahedron using Polydron shapes.

A dodecahedron has:

_____ regular pentagon faces

_____ corners

_____ edges

LDA

POLYDRON

The Icosahedron

Here is a drawing of an icosahedron.

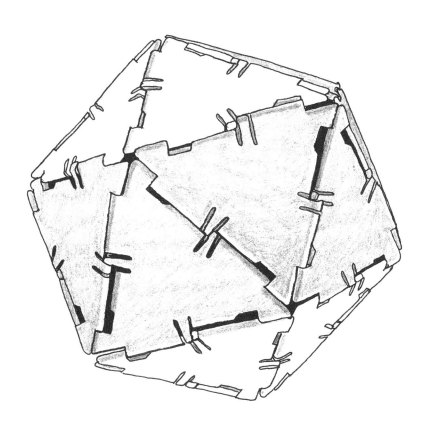

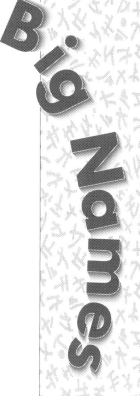

Make an icosahedron using Polydron shapes.

An icosahedron has:

_____ equilateral triangle faces

_____ corners

_____ edges

Truncated Tetrahedron

Truncated solids are made by cutting the corners off some other solid.

Tick which of these you think is a truncated tetrahedron.

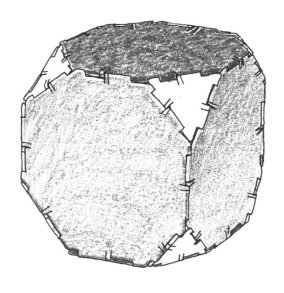
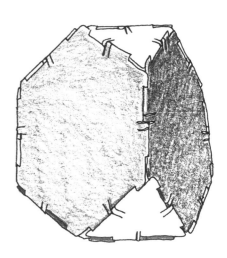

Make a truncated tetrahedron from Polydron shapes.

Here is part of the net for a truncated tetrahedron.

Draw in the missing pieces.

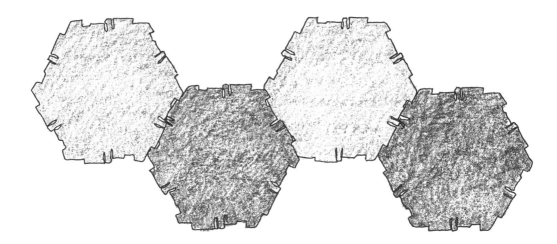

LDA

POLYDRON

Truncated Cube

Truncated solids are made by cutting the corners off another 3D shape.

Tick which of these you think is a truncated cube.

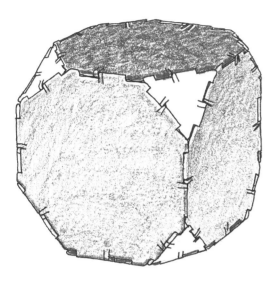 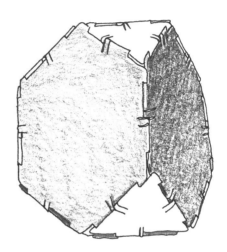

Make a truncated cube from Polydron shapes.

Here is part of the net for a truncated cube.

Draw in the missing pieces.

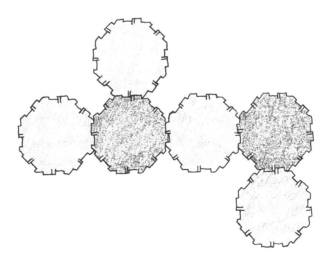

LDA

POLYDRON

The Cuboctahedron

Here is a drawing of a cuboctahedron.

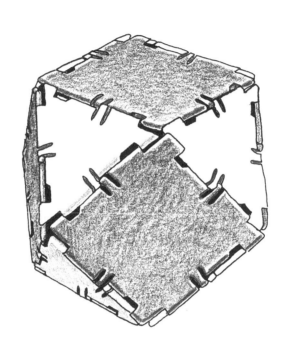

Make a cuboctahedron using Polydron shapes.

A cuboctahedron has:

_____ square faces

_____ equilateral triangle faces

_____ corners

_____ edges

LDA

POLYDRON

The Rhombicuboctahedron

Here is a drawing of a rhombicuboctahedron.

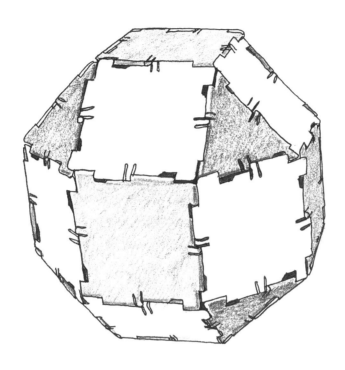

Make a rhombicuboctahedron using Polydron shapes.

A rhombicuboctahedron has:

_____ square faces

_____ equilateral triangle faces

_____ corners

_____ edges

LDA   POLYDRON

teacher's notes

Shape Allsorts

The main focus of these activities is to consider shapes which are slightly 'different' in some way. For example shapes which have no symmetry, concave shapes and shapes which lean to one side.

Teaching opportunities

Discuss ways in which a solid shape can be described, such as:

> number of faces, edges and corners
> the shapes of the faces
> whether all the faces are exactly the same shape and size
> whether the shape is symmetrical

Discuss ways in which flat shapes can be described, such as:

> number of sides
> whether it is symmetrical
> concave or convex sides
> size of angles

Challenges

Drawing a complete solid shape can be challenging. The shapes of the faces can be drawn with the number of each indicated.

Discuss classification of solids, such as:

> prisms
> pyramids
> complex shapes – made up from two or more different solid shapes.
> truncated solids – ones which have one or more corners removed.

Make examples of these solid shapes.

No Symmetry

Clip pairs of Polydron shapes together.

The new shapes you make must not be symmetrical.

Draw some of your non-symmetrical shapes.

LDA

POLYDRON

Leaning Pyramids

Make a pyramid.

Your pyramid must lean to one side.

Try to make different leaning pyramids.

Draw the shapes you used to make each leaning pyramid.

LDA

POLYDROH

Strange Prisms

Make some prisms.

The end of each prism must not be symmetrical.

Draw the ends of the prisms you made.

LDA

POLYDRON

![shape Allsorts](vertical sidebar text)

Concave solids

Concave faces point inwards.

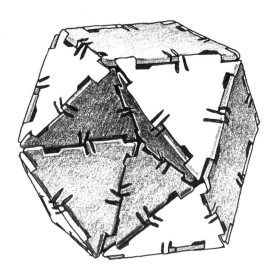

Make a solid shape which has concave faces.

Draw or describe your concave shape.

LDA

POLYDRON

Concave shapes

Concave 2D shapes have sides which re-enter the shape.

Here is a concave hexagon.

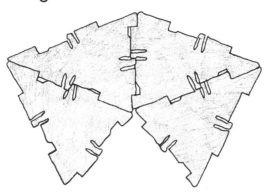

Clip Polydron pieces together to make other concave shapes.

Draw or describe some of your concave shapes.

LDA

POLYDRON

Meeting point

These sets of 2D shapes all meet together at a point.

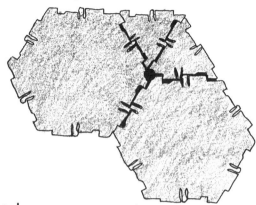

Make your own sets of 2D shapes which meet at a point.

Draw some of your shapes.

LDA

POLYDRON

Shape Allsorts

Shape Challenge

Make an interesting solid shape.

Try to make each face look different.

Write about your solid shape and draw the faces.

POLYDRON

POLYDRON

This Book
Belongs To Me

_____

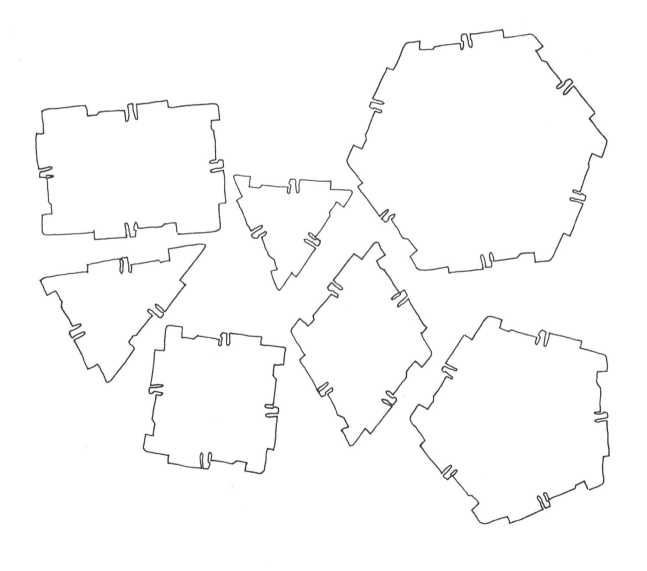